T0368434

The World of
Grace O'Malley

The World of Grace O'Malley:

Irish Mistress of the Seas

by

Elizabeth O'Maley

AuthorHouse™
1663 Liberty Drive
Bloomington, IN 47403
www.authorhouse.com
Phone: 1 (800) 839-8640

Published by AuthorHouse 11/10/2015

ISBN: 978-1-5049-5918-6 (sc)
ISBN: 978-1-5049-5919-3 (e)

Library of Congress Control Number: 2015918023

Print information available on the last page.

Any people depicted in stock imagery provided by Thinkstock are models,
and such images are being used for illustrative purposes only.
Certain stock imagery © Thinkstock.

This book is printed on acid-free paper.

authorHOUSE®

For Larry, Amy, Laurie, Carrie, Mark, Isaac,
Salma, Corbin, Carter, and all the O'Maleys

May you sail through life with the wind at your back,
sheltered from storms
by the love of your family.

Laurie O'Maley Shipchandler and children view the sea
from a distant shore, Santorini, Greece.

Grace O'Malley was a sea captain and clan leader, pirate and politico, business woman and warrior, as well as a dutiful daughter, wife, and mother. Though shaped by her times, she shattered the mold for women of her day. She would be a formidable figure in any era, including our own.

Part of the sea-faring O'Malley clan, she inherited a deep love of the oceans and dominated trade on the Irish coast. On land, she personally led her clansmen in battle, waging relentless war on rival leaders throughout the Emerald Isle. Even powerful English officials were threatened by her influence. They saw her as "nurse to all rebellions."

When she went to London to meet the Queen of England, the two women dealt as proud equals who had maneuvered their way through 16ᵗʰ century war and politics with skill and aplomb.

Enter now the world of Grace O'Malley.

"Pirates"

I am Granuaile Ni O Maille. You may know me as Grainne or Grace O'Malley, the Pirate Queen. In the end, I care not what you call me. I wish you to know me by my deeds.

Grace O'Malley, as depicted in diorama at
Grace O'Malley Exhibition in Louisburg, County Mayo

I was born in the west of Ireland in the year 1530. Ireland was just a speck of green land in the midst of endless sea. Many felt imprisoned by its walls of waves. But not the O'Malleys! The sea freed us. By the time of my birth, the O'Malleys had ruled the western waters for many generations. My people were known in all Ireland as "the lions of the green sea."

Map of Ireland from 1592 by Abraham Ortelius

My father was chieftain of our clan. The people called him "Black Oak" for his great strength. He ruled the kingdom of Umhall in the province of Connaught. His land wrapped round Clew Bay, including its many islands. It is said our bay has 365 islands, one for each day of the year.

Within our kingdom lay Crough Patrick. Do you not know of it? It is the holiest mountain in all Ireland. It was at its peak that St. Patrick fasted in solitude for forty days and nights.

Then, from that sacred place, he blessed the people of Ireland and declared no poisonous snake should ever inhabit our Isle.

Each year I was able, I made the climb to the top with my followers to honor Patrick. From the summit, I could survey our kingdom and view the islands of the bay. On a clear day, it was a glorious sight!

Clew Bay from statue of Saint Patrick on Crough Patrick

Our kingdom was beautiful, full of hills and rivers, lakes and streams. But I loved best the craggy coastline. My father had many castles there to protect his land from foreign invaders as well as rival Irish chieftains.

Craggy Coast of Achill

Beauty of County Mayo

Near Louisburg, County Mayo

My mother was Margaret. She was queen of Black Oak's castles. Though our towers repelled our enemies, many friends passed through our doors. My parents were known for their great hospitality. Nary a stranger left our home hungry. As a powerful chieftain, my father owned a large herd of cattle, so great platters of meat were always on our tables. After the evening meal, musicians and bards entertained us.

Meal and Entertainment, by John Derricke

But unlike most Irish chieftains, my father's riches were not confined to livestock and land. Black Oak's wealth came from the sea. He held the largest fleet of ships in all Ireland, from which he controlled trade on the whole west coast. He forced Galway merchants to pay tolls to sail goods through his waters. He charged foreign traders to guide their boats through dangerous currents, past treacherous rocks and reefs. If they failed to pay, he would board their ships and seize the bounty. In this way, he enforced his terms.

His largest ships were galleys. They could easily carry two hundred men. With them, he transported gallowglass from Scotland. Gallowglass were fierce fighting men, paid by warring chieftains to fill their armies.

But my father's most profitable voyages were made to trade in foreign lands. He would leave for Spain carrying herring and hides and return with wine and rich fabrics desired by wealthy lords.

A Herring Trawler by Gerrit
Groenewegen, 1789

A Galley as carved on tomb in MacDufie's
Chapel in Oronsay, 1772

Gallowglass

As a young child, I climbed the steep hills near our castle at Kildownet on the island of Achill. From the cliffs, I watched the boats on the bay and surveyed my father's more distant islands. As I looked toward the sea, I wondered, "Does the sea go on forever, or is there land like ours on the other side?"

The sea's reply was in the wind. "Come away with me, come away with me," she whispered.

View from Achill

My brother already sailed with my father. But I knew he couldn't hear the voice of the sea as plainly as me. Perhaps nobody did. I decided I must convince my father to take me, too.

It was no small thing to change his mind. He said I was too small. And I was a girl. A ship was no place for a woman, especially one not yet ten. According to Black Oak O'Malley, my place was at home in the castle. But I had my father's blood, and I believe he sensed my love of the sea.

He agreed to take me on fishing expeditions in the bay, and in time, on wild open waters. I became an eager student of tides and currents, rocks and shoals, astrolabes and starry night skies. I trained myself to divine every small change of weather. In this way I earned the respect of the men on the ship, and more importantly, the praise of my father.

Durer Star Chart, 1515

Astrolabe Ring

Within a year, I found myself aboard his galley heading to Spain. Seville was like no place I'd been before. So many ships were at its docks! Such gold and riches on display! My desire for foreign shores only increased. That voyage was the start of my life as mistress of the seas.

Seville, Spain in 16th century, busiest port in Europe as center of trade between Old and New World

But to my dismay, my young seafaring days were cut short. At fifteen, my father decided I must marry. He found me an excellent match, Donal of the Battles O'Flaherty. The union profited both our clans. Though I didn't wish to marry, I was proud to advance my family's interests. The land of the O'Flahertys adjoined our own and stretched all the way to Galway Bay and Lough Corrib. Donal was known as an eager fighter and would doubtless protect and expand our holdings. My father hoped his strong temper might curb my own.

We married at Murrisk Abbey. The Abbey was founded by his family in the century before my birth. Murrisk lay at the base of Crough Patrick and was the starting point for our yearly pilgrimage to the top. It was the perfect place to begin my marriage, in the O'Malley Abbey by the sea, in the shadow of Crough Patrick.

Murrisk Abbey, 1792

In five years time, our marriage produced a daughter and two sons. They were my hopes for the future. I named the girl Margaret, for my mother, and the boys, Owen and Murrough. My old seafaring life seemed just a dream. As any mother, I loved my children but grew restless as I gazed at the sea from Donal's castle. The wind still called "Come away with me. Come away with me."

Dingle Harvest by Gerry Dillon

Soon fate danced by and spun my life toward my desires. My husband was a battling man and couldn't keep peace with the neighboring Joyces. They held a castle on the lonely rock island in the midst of Lough Corrib. Kirk Castle was a formidable fortress, inaccessible by land, with slippery sloped walls as thick as a man is tall. The bards say it was built by a magical cock and hen.

Kirk Castle

Donal believed the castle should be his. He attacked and seized it. The castle was then called Cock's Castle in honor of his bravery. The Joyces responded with a revenge attack, and Donal died. With Donal gone, they returned once more, hoping for an easy victory. I knew I must defend the castle to protect my children and avenge my husband's death. On land as well as on sea, I was my father's daughter. I rallied my husband's clansmen and led them in battle. The castle was saved. In my honor they renamed it Hen's Castle. From then on, Donal's clansmen followed me.

Kern attack by John Derricke

Hen's Castle

Freed by widowhood, I returned to my father's kingdom of Umhall. I received the lands of my mother and settled into my castle on Clare Island. Donal's kinsman came along, giving me a fine fighting force of loyal kern. When my father died, I assumed control of the O'Malley fleet. To establish my authority, I attacked castles of rival clans all up and down the coast. I dominated my foes both on land and water, building a secure and prosperous life for my family. And I was free to follow the song of the sea.

Clare Island, Clew Bay.

Clare Island from shore of Clew Bay

At the age of 36, I chose to take a second husband, Richard-in-Iron Bourke. I felt he had a promising future. If we joined our might together, he might become the MacWilliam, the most powerful man in Mayo. I also desired possession of his Carraigahowley (Rockfleet) Castle. Secluded on a hidden inlet of the bay, it was less vulnerable than my Clare Island home. I quickly moved my forces there. And that is where I remained the rest of my days.

My new husband allowed me great freedom, for his success was furthered by mine. I spent much time at sea, trading where I could, plundering when I must. Tales of my ventures were repeated at the English court, even to the queen herself.

When possible, I left the tumult on land for the pleasures of the sea. Deep waters continued to call me, sometimes in low whispers, sometimes in howling cries. I even gave birth at sea. My son Theobold was born on a galley in the year 1567 and known as Toby-of-the-Ship. He fell heir to all my dreams.

Carraigahowley (Rockfleet) Castle

The day following his birth, our galley was attacked by ferocious Barbary pirates, the most notorious men at sea. These unholy raiders came from north Africa and for years had raided the coastlines and isles of lands near and far. They were known to slaughter thousands of victims a day, and haul the survivors to Africa as slaves. While nursing Toby below, I could hear my men screaming in terror. Some threw themselves into the briny depths, more willing to die than be captured.

I couldn't allow my newborn son to lose his life or his freedom. Though weak from childbirth, I climbed up on deck to rally my crew. Shouting a blistering oath, I swung my saber with all my might, cutting down three corsairs with a single blow. I emptied my musket into the belly of an escaping wretch, while berating my men for lack of courage. Spurred on by my example, my men uttered a battle cry and took up my cause. Never again would they give up a fight, even a hopeless one.

A Battle with Barbary Pirates

The English were determined to control all Ireland. They blamed me for disturbing the peace. They brought governors and armies into Mayo to restore order. But I remained determined to advance the prospects of my family and was willing to fight or deal with either English lords or Irish chieftains to get my way. My life was like the games of chance I loved to play. I'd carefully calculate my move, then let the dice fly.

I met with the English Lord Deputy, Sir Henry Sidney, in Galway. Both he and his son were mightily impressed with me.

English Army marches through Ireland, by John Derricke

When my husband agreed to rule by English law and supply a goodly number of men for the army, he was knighted. We became a Lord and his Lady, allied with the power of the English crown. This bond was a great boon to our ambitions.

Submission to English crown before Sir Henry Sidney,
by John Derricke

A rich and influential chieftain to our south, The Earl of Desmond, controlled a vast amount of land. To counter his prestige, I invaded his territory and plundered his castles.

I paid dearly for this venture. He captured me and threw me in Limerick Jail. He then turned me over to English officials as proof of his own loyalty to the crown. I was imprisoned in Dublin Castle. I cannot fully express the pain of my lost years of freedom. My daughter's husband, the Devil's Hook, finally secured my release.

Tower of Dublin Castle where Grace was imprisoned, 1910 postcard

But our friends and foes were constantly changing. My husband then joined my jailer Desmond to fight the English. Unlucky Desmond was murdered in revenge and his head delivered to Queen Elizabeth who displayed it on London Bridge.

Murder of Earl of Desmond by English, from Cassell's History of England, *1857*

Throughout the rest of my days, my foulest enemy was the English governor of Connaught, Richard Bingham. He was as cruel and treacherous as any Barbary pirate. He plundered my land, stole my cattle, slaughtered the women and children in my care, and murdered my son Owen. In 1593 he seized Toby and charged him with treason. I feared he'd put Toby to death. I was now an impoverished old widow and couldn't bear the loss of another son. What was I to do?

Again, the sea spoke. "Come with me," she crooned. I sailed my ship to London to present my case to the English queen. I would not let Bingham stop me. I navigated the coast through all my secret places. I steered up the busy Thames River, undaunted by the wide-eyed heads of pirates, traitors, madmen, and thieves.

Thames River and Old London Bridge

I met the queen at her palace at Greenwich. Never had I seen such splendor of costume and jewels. But I had not come to admire this woman's riches. I had come to demand justice. She was no better a woman than me. Though she might command a formidable navy, she had never steered a ship through howling winds. She had never stormed a castle or fought a fusilier.

I appealed to her as a woman of grit like herself, who had spent a lifetime fulfilling duties to family, followers, and God. I asked that she free my innocent son and allow me to support myself by trade as an independent woman on land and sea.

Bingham denied all wrong-doing and accused me of many crimes. But the queen stood by me. She ordered Bingham to set Toby free and allow me to live by my trade. Her rebuke of my arch enemy brought me much satisfaction.

Grace O'Malley meets Queen Elizabeth

Now an old woman, my hopes for the future rest with my children and theirs. They will carry my dreams down through the years. I hope that like me, they will hear the voice of the sea, claim their freedom, and strike out for distant shores. I know there is always one more.

Atlantic Drive, Achill by Gerry Dillon

The details of Grace O'Malley's death are unclear, but it is thought she died at Rockfleet Castle about 1603. She was involved in trade, war, and politics until the end. Elizabeth of England died at Richmond Palace the same year. Grace is said to be interred in the O'Malley family crypt in the Cisterian Abbey on Clare Island. Though her world has passed from earth into memory, it may still be glimpsed in her castle ruins, the scenery of Mayo, and views of the endless sea.

Cisterian Abbey on Clare Island, reputed final resting place of Grace O'Malley

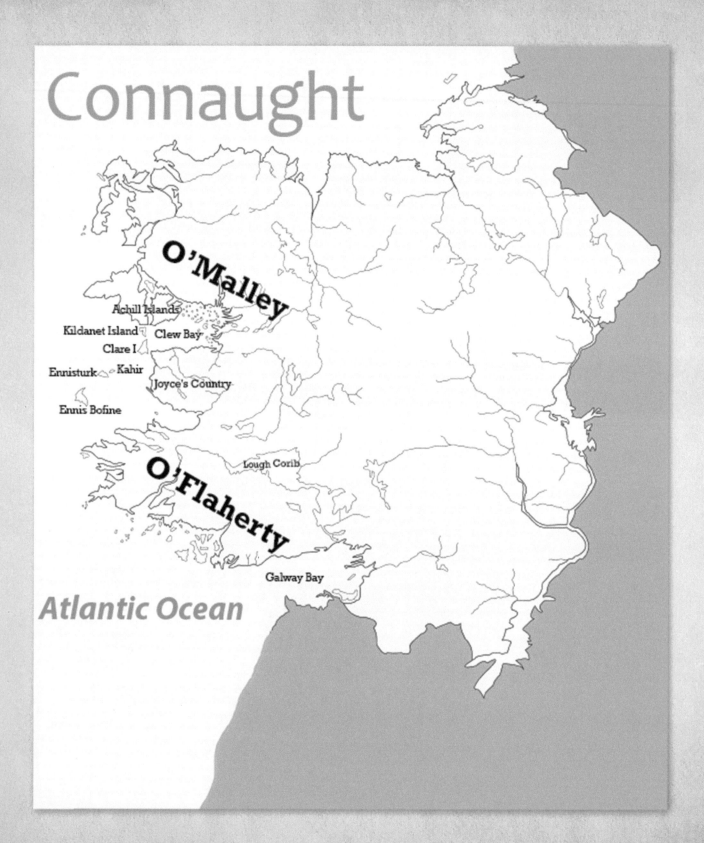

Connaught

O'Malley

Achill Islands

Kildanet Island

Clare I

Clew Bay

Ennisturk

Kahir

Joyce's Country

Ennis Bofine

Lough Corib

O'Flaherty

Galway Bay

Atlantic Ocean

Author

Elizabeth O'Maley lives in Fort Wayne, Indiana with her husband Larry. They have four adult children and three grandchildren. Like Grace O'Malley, they all love traveling and exploring new places. They don't know if they are descended from Grace, but enjoy imagining it!

Elizabeth is a graduate of Miami University in Oxford, Ohio with a BA in Political Science and a MS in School Psychology. She has two previously published books, *By Freedom's Light* (Indiana Historical Society, 2009) and *Bones on the Ground* (Indiana Historical Society, 2014).

The World of Grace O'Malley: Irish Mistress of the Seas began as a gift to my family in celebration of their Irish heritage. Special thanks to my husband Larry for traveling up and down the west coast of Ireland with me in search of Grace, to Carrie O'Maley Voliva for help preparing the manuscript, to Andy O' Maley and Kenny Cook for help creating maps, to artist Gerry Dillon of Limerick for use of his paintings, and to Grace O'Malley for speaking so strongly to my imagination.

Editor's Note: Elizabeth O'Maley died on May 20, 2014.

Elizabeth O'Maley visits Clew Bay

Recommended Further Reading and Sources

Books

Author Anne Chambers is the leading authority on the life of Grace O'Malley. Her books include *Ireland's Pirate Queen: The True Story of Grace O'Malley* (MFJ Books, New York, 2003.), *Granuaile: Sea Queen of Ireland* (The Collins Press, Cork, 2006.), *Shadow Lord: Theobold Bourke, Tibbott-ne-Long, Son of the Pirate Queen, Grace O'Malley,* (Ashfield Press, Dublin, 2007.)

Gerstl, Hugo. *Amazing Grace: The Story of Grace O'Malley the Notorious Pirate Woman* (Dekel Publishing House, Israel, 2011)

Derricke, John. *The Image of Irelande, with Discourie of Woodkarne* (Edinbourgh, 1783.)

Faulkner, Matt. *The Pirate Meets the Queen* (a children's picture book), (Philomel Books, New York, 2005.)

Lonely Planet Ireland

Malloy, Sheila. *O'Malley* (Ballinakella Press, Whitegate, Co. Clare, 1998.)

Websites

www.graceomalley.com

www.discoverireland.ie/places-to-go

www.clewbay.net/clew-bay-geography-heritage

www.clewbay.net/video

Printed in the United States
by Baker & Taylor Publisher Services